GAUGUIN.

The life and work of the artist illustrated with 80 colour plates

GIUSEPPE MARCHIORI

THAMES AND HUDSON

Translated from the Italian by Caroline Beamish

This edition © 1968 Thames and Hudson, 30-34 Bloomsbury Street, London WC 1

Copyright © 1967 by Sadea Editore, Firenze

Printed in Italy

Life

The picture of Gauguin can be pieced together from self-portraits and from letters, read in conjunction with one another; the painted and the written word help to bring alive a face that has been altered by the passage of time. His most recent biographers have discovered photographs, too, to assist us. The strongly modelled face, with its deep furrows, is the mirror of a personality which can never be completely disguised by the distortions and falsifications of a novel or a film.

His inner life, intense, rich, profound, was lived in far greater secrecy than one might gather from the famous and spectacularly violent episodes connnected with it such as the extraordinary climax of his friendship with Van Gogh in Arles, when Van Gogh, without premeditation, sliced off his ear. More important facts about his life concern his vocation for the exotic, in life as in art; the building up of his personality as a superman, beyond all normal emotional and moral ties; his complete withdrawal from society and from his bourgeois background; the blindly egoistic choice of freedom and solitude inspired by his almost super-human pride.

His taste for the exotic and for adventure began with the voyages he made in his early youth. The sailor boy was running away from bourgeois civilization in search of the island of his dreams, an earthly paradise created by his imagination. He dreamed of countries where time had stood still in some primordial age of truth and innocence; distant lands where he could leave his ship and find salvation.

In February 1889, in a letter to his wife, Gauguin gave the finishing touch to his ideal picture of himself by admitting that he had made the choice between his sensitive and his primitive nature and had chosen to follow the latter, which he maintained would allow him to progress firmly and without hesitation.

Paul Gauguin was born in Paris on 7 June 1848. His father, Clovis, was a journalist on the *National*. His mother, Aline

Marie Chazal, was the daughter of Flora Tristan, a woman famous for propagating socialism and social studies who had spent her lifetime wandering about France.

Flora Tristan was the illegitimate daughter of Don Mariano de Tristan y Moscoso (who died in 1807), a member of an Aragonese family which had emigrated to Peru and become one of the richest and most influential families in the country. Having run away from her husband, the engraver André Chazal, Flora spent long periods in Europe and America. One day in 1838, the couple met by chance and had a violent quarrel, during which Chazal wounded his wife severely and was sentenced to twenty years hard labour as a result. Flora ended her restless life in Bordeaux in 1844.

In 1849 Clovis Gauguin, violently opposing the régime established by Louis Napoleon, decided to leave for Peru with his wife and two children, Paul and Marie. But the unfortunate Clovis died on 30 October 1849, in the Straits of Magellan, and his widow had to continue her journey to Lima alone with the two children.

Gauguin spent his childhood, until 1855, in the princely household of the Tristan y Moscoso family in Lima; the memory of that period was to stay with him for ever. On their return to France he was sent to the seminary of Orleans, where he began his regular studies.

He was a reserved, silent, irritable child, disliked by everybody. ' I believe I learnt, during my childhood and in that seminary, to hate hypocrisy, double dealing and sneaking (*semper tres*), and to distrust anything that ran contrary to my instinct, heart and reason. '

These words were written by Gauguin, and they throw a lot of light on the formation of his character, completing the portrait of the exile with a touch of that realism which he normally so fiercely rejected.

His haughty independence was a romantic reaction to the manners and thought of the day. His escape began on 7 December 1865, when the seventeen year old Gauguin boarded the *Luzitan*, bound for Rio de Janeiro, as a cabinboy. The voyage began at the end of October 1866 with the ship going from port to port, working its way backwards and forwards between South America and Le Havre, where the young sailor disembarked in December 1867. In the meanwhile his mother had died in July 1867 at Saint Cloud, far from her son who loved her devotedly; in 1890 he painted a portrait of her, from a daguerreotype, which conveyed the true distinction of her aristocratic beauty.

In 1868 Gauguin went to sea again, as a third-class sailor on the ' Jérôme Napoléon ', a yacht with a crew of 150 men, owned by Jerome Napoleon, and his wife, Clothilde de Savoie, daughter of Vittorio Emanuele II. During one cruise, in May 1869, Gauguin visited Trieste and Venice. The yacht, with Prince Jerome Napoleon on board, was sailing away to some unnamed island in the sun when the Prussians invaded France and the Napoleonic Empire collapsed in fragments.

Gauguin returned to France and became a peaceful bourgeois citizen; on 22 November 1873 he married a rich young Danish girl, Mette Gad, and had five children by her. He showed great ability as a stockbroker; he even managed to put together a choice collection of impressionist paintings after having begun to paint himself, purely as a hobby. As the years passed his passion for painting grew and grew and he decided in 1883 to give up his job and to move to Rouen, where life was less expensive. In November 1884 growing financial difficulties forced him to depart with his family for Denmark but, after a few months, incompatibility with the bourgeois ways of the Gad family irritated him to such a pitch that he decided to leave for Paris with his son Clovis.

The winter of 1885 was a terrible one. Gauguin worked as a billposter in order to live, and struggled desperately against adversity. Clovis, who was delicate, became ill. His father lost hope of ever overcoming his penury, or of finding a foothold in Parisian artistic circles.

In June 1886 he departed for Brittany and stayed at Pont-Aven, where he got to know Emile Bernard; in November he returned to Paris and met Van Gogh. On 10 April 1887 he and the painter Charles Laval set sail for Martinique, stopping at Panama to earn enough money to continue their voyage by working as labourers on the digging of the canal.

In December 1887, exhausted by sickness and indigence, Gauguin returned to France.

When Daniel de Monfreid saw him for the first time, in December 1887, Gauguin had only just returned from his disastrous journey to Martinique (more of an inferno than a heaven upon earth); already the nature of the person he was to become was in striking evidence. Monfreid, with some psychological insight, described him in these words: 'His manner is haughty, his gaze penetrating, diffident, enigmatic yet questioning, his mouth tightly closed in mysterious silence; he arouses no sympathy in me. In addition, his views on art, put forward in a peremptory tone, seemed questionable. Lastly the paintings that I saw looked horrible.'

His first attempt was a failure. Distant countries were a literary invention. Mallarmé had written *Lève l'ancre pour une exotique nature*, and Gauguin had set sail, confessing: 'I am two things which can never be held up to ridicule: a child and a savage.'

His absurd, seemingly delirious hopefulness and romanticism were supported by unyielding obstinacy. So, after another visit to Brittany where he taught art to a group of young men, Gauguin left for Tahiti on 4 April 1891 with money raised by an exhibition at the Hôtel Drouot; the show was a success thanks to two favourable reviews by Octave Mirbeau.

Tahiti was an immediate disappointment. Papeete, the capital, was ruled by officials, clerks and soldiers, like a little French sub-prefecture only even more narrow minded and boring. Gauguin was thought to be on some government mission and was regarded with some suspicion as a spy. When poverty forced him to go and live in a native village, miserable about the difficulty of communicating with Paris, embittered by his clashes with colonial authority, drinking far too much, surrounded by Tahitian girls who 'invaded his bed', Gauguin was ostracized by Papeete society and was virtually forced to return to France. After a long and exhausting voyage under conditions which only a man as strong as he was could have survived, Gauguin disembarked at Marseilles in August 1893 without a penny to his name.

An old uncle in Orleans died at this time, leaving Gauguin a legacy which was just sufficient to instal him in Paris with a half-Malay girl, Javanese Annah, and then to take him to Brittany to take up his mission as prophet of the new syntheticist movement once again. In a brawl with some sailors, who had mocked his girl friend, his ankle was fractured; in the forced immobility which followed he spent the last of his legacy and once again found himself destitute. His studio in Paris had been ransacked by the mulatto girl who had left him in Brittany. This train of disasters culminated in his final break with Mette, whom he had gone to visit in Copenhagen. In Paris no one took him seriously as an artist, though his haughty mien and his wild, mysterious gaze made people afraid of his sarcasm and of the violence with which he voiced his theories. His friends organized another public sale for him, but it did not do as well as was expected, in spite of the letter from Strindberg that was printed in the catalogue (18 February 1895). Gauguin decided to depart as soon as possible. In March 1895 for the second and last time he embarked on a boat that would take him straight to Tahiti.

He stayed in Tahiti for seven years. His letters to Daniel de Monfreid give some idea of his life, of the privation, the toil, the struggles, the extravagances, the obsessive eroticism, the physical and mental anguish, the uncertainty, the futile arguments, the blighted harvest of his wounded pride and his thwarted seeking for power. But Gauguin himself believed in his paintings and considered himself a genius ('I am a great artist and I know it'), and he hated the men who had betrayed his trust, like Emile Bernard. To Schuffenecker, who had advised him, when he was in particularly desperate straits, to apply to the State for assistance, Gauguin replied with great dignity that he would never beg nor give up his independence by asking for help.

As the days passed and his physical condition deteriorated (he suffered from syphilis, contracted in Paris before his return to Tahiti, and from the fractured ankle which had never healed and which gave him terrible pain), and as his financial troubles grew (though he exaggerated them in his letters for fear of destitution), Gauguin fell into a black depression. He attempted suicide in 1897.

'This voyage to Tahiti is a mad, a sad and a hideous adventure. I can only think of death which frees us from all suffering', he confessed to his friend Monfreid. And he added: 'the older I get the less civilized I become.'

He went on from Tahiti to a remoter refuge, Hiva Oa in the Marquesas Islands, in search of somewhere completely uncivilized where he could forget his past life. Gauguin was by now quite cut off from the world in which he had lived and struggled, even though the canvases he sent to Europe constituted some kind of poetic message (understood by very few). The 'right to dare anything' had cost him all he had. In 1897 Aline, his favourite daughter, had died; she was the only member of his family who did not seem to be alienated by his hungry face, marked as it was by a struggle, carried on against everybody and everything, including his own emotions, to affirm his artistic personality and his destiny as a painter. At this time of desperation, Gauguin painted the great frieze entitled *Where do we come from? What are we? Where are we going?*

On his departure from Marseilles on 3 July 1895, Gauguin wrote to Charles Morice: 'There is nothing left for me but to dig my grave out there, amongst the silence and the flowers.' The idea of death persecuted him, and he did nothing to prevent its coming.

At Hiva Oa he continued his polemical writings, begun in Tahiti. In *Guêpes* and in successive issues of *Sourire*, he attacked officials for exploiting the natives. He had become a defender of the natives of the island, and continued to associate with them freely, particularly the women; this caused great annoyance to the gendarmerie, the supreme authority of the island, and scandalized the Catholic missionaries who considered him both corrupt and a corrupting influence.

Through the long Polynesian nights, plagued by insomnia, Gauguin thought, painted and wrote. His only constant companions were Tioka, his native servant, and the Protestant pastor Vernier. From 1900 onwards, Vollard sent regular monthly payments, and money was paid into his account

with the Société Générale by the remarkable Monfreid. Gau
guin went on talking about debts and straitened circumstances, but his circumstances in Hiva Oa were not in fact so
desperate. The last three years of his life were embittered
less by his shortage of money than by the worsening of
his disease, his own intransigence and his obstinate ina-
bility to distinguish between the loftiest artistic problems
and the petty local squabbles which were inflamed by his
humanitarian feelings, his love of justice and his combative
temperament.

One day, when he seemed to have come to the end of his
physical and mental energy, Gauguin wrote to Daniel de
Monfreid that he wished he could return to France. But his
friend advised him against it, in a letter full of admiration
for the painter (who in spite of his praise remained uncon-
vinced).

'You have now become an extraordinary, legendary figure
among painters, sending your disconcerting and inimitable
pictures from those distant islands; your paintings are those
of a great man who has disappeared (or so it seems) from
the face of the earth. Your enemies (and there are plenty
of them, as there always are for those who annoy the bourgeois) do not say anything and do not dare to attack you
– it does not even occur to them because you are so far
away. You must not come back: you enjoy the immunity
of the great dead; you have become part of the history
of art.'

Perhaps kindly Monfreid was exaggerating, spurred on by
friendship and admiration. But his judgment was shared
by the young who, even if they did not appreciate Gauguin's paintings fully, had at any rate understood them.
In 1897 Gauguin wrote to Daniel de Monfreid: 'I want
only silence, silence and more silence. I want to be left
to die in peace, forgotten, and if I must go on living let
it be in peace, forgotten. What does it matter if I am the
pupil of Sérusier or Bernard? If I have created something
beautiful nothing will hide the fact; but if my paintings
are rubbish then why try and gild them, why try and pull
the wool over people's eyes by pretending they are worth
something? At any rate society can never accuse me of

having robbed them of much money with false pretences.'
The 'House of Pleasure' (the choice of name, a bitter
unintentional irony, was intended as a challenge to the
missionaries, whom Gauguin thought hypocrites) opened its
doors to young prostitutes; and Gauguin, inflamed with
alcohol and morphine, fancied he loved them all, just as
during the first years of his return to a primitive life. But
at other moments he would say to himself: 'Now it is
night. Everything sleeps. My eyes gaze, without compre-
hending, at dreams in the infinite space that used to lie
before me. I have the sweet sensation of the sad path of
my disappointed hope.'

His excited imagination relived in painted landscapes and
figures the vicissitudes of his wandering life, now nearly
at its close. The cabin boy who had sailed to Rio had
become a melancholy old man, quarrelsome and degenerate,
the enemy of the Europeans who had betrayed his ideals.
'The savage is certainly better than we are,' he wrote to
Charles Morice. 'You made a mistake when you said once
that I was wrong to call myself a savage. It's true – I am
a savage. And civilized people understand it intuitively
since what surprises and upsets them in my paintings is
a savage quality which is there in spite of my efforts to
suppress it, and which is inimitable.'

Condemned again for his protest against the sufferings of
a group of natives, Gauguin shut himself up in the 'House
of Pleasure', cared for by Tioka and comforted by the
visits of Pastor Vernier. Vernier listened with astonishment
to Gauguin's disquieting monologues in which he expounded
his revolutionary theories about art and memories of his
adventurous life. This went on until the month of May
1903. Then his pains grew worse, his spirit was distracted
by the nightmares he suffered when he was alone, by the
visions of nights made endless by insomnia, by the on-
slaughts of troubled memories. On 8 May he collapsed with
heart failure; alone, he hid himself away like a wild beast,
to die away from prying eyes. He was buried in the mission
cemetery, and on his plain tombstone, until a few years
ago, could be found a circle of red clay on which Tioka had
cut the words 'PAUL GAUGUIN 1903'.

After more than sixty years a few words might be added to that inscription, words that he wrote himself shortly before he died: 'I have worked well, and used my life well, even intelligently, and with courage.'

Works

Maurice Malingue, after years of research, has succeeded in correcting a series of fallacies about Gauguin's beginnings as a painter, and clearing away the legends which have grown up around these fallacies.

The second-class seaman, Paul Gauguin, who had left his ship on 23 April 1871, went straight to St Cloud to look for his mother's house, destroyed during the war; he found his sister Marie-Marcelline, who had been given a home by her teacher Gustave Arosa, with whom she stayed until her marriage in 1875. Arosa was passionately devoted to art and possessed a collection of paintings by Delacroix, Daumier, Courbet, Corot, Jongkind and Pissarro.

Gauguin was unemployed. Arosa's son-in-law got him a job with Bertin, a stockbroker, but his true vocation was painting. In fact by this time (1871) he had already begun to paint regularly, not intermittently like the usual 'Sunday painter'. There exists in Copenhagen, in the Ny Carlsberg Glyptotek, a painting by him entitled *House by a Lake* painted in oils on paper, which shows the influence of Corot. Marie Heegaard has recorded that Gauguin used to paint at St Cloud with Marguerite, Arosa's daughter, and Marie was often their model. Later he attended a course at the Académie Colarossi. In 1880, at Arosa's house, he met Pissarro, who, by his teaching and example, contributed to the formation of Gauguin's art.

Gauguin was a talented stockbroker, and supported his family with ease. The real reason he continued to work was because this made it possible for him to buy paintings that he liked (Manet, Cézanne, Renoir, Sisley, Pissarro, Monet and Guillaumin) and to spend moments of leisure painting.

In 1886 he showed seven paintings in the fifth impressionist exhibition. The man whom people regarded as a

'Sunday painter' was already a mature artist; he had already painted *The Seine at the Pont d'Iéna* (*pl. 1*) in 1875, a white scene much closer to Guillaumin than to Monet and, in 1880, the *Study of a Nude, or Suzanne sewing* (*pl. 2*) which has the plastic strength of a Courbet but departs from reality – i.e. Gauguin constructs a nude figure which is far removed from naturalism (Huysmans himself called him a naturalist), and which is already close to the style defined by René Huyghe as expressionism.

Impressionism for Gauguin meant the painting of Pissarro, with its colours minutely fragmented to catch the subtlest shifting of light and shade. And he remained faithful to Pissarro for years, with a momentary lapse in the *Study of a Nude*, an isolated premonition of what was to happen later in his Brittany and Tahiti periods.

In 1881, in Pissarro's house in Osny, Gauguin met Cézanne. On a human level this encounter was without sequel. The 'bourgeois' of Aix was not made to understand someone like Gauguin: many years later he was to say acrimoniously: 'Gauguin had carried his little sensation round all the steamships.'

Gauguin on the other hand was fascinated by the painting of Cézanne, which seemed to him to contain hints of the near future, when impressionism would be nothing more than a memory. Albert Aurier noted that Gauguin had flattened out Cézanne's relief modelling. In a letter to Schuffenecker, written on 14 January 1885, Gauguin demonstrates how well he understood the misunderstood Cézanne, who 'loves the mystery and motionless peace of the figure of a man lying dreaming on the ground. His colours are as serious as the oriental character. A southerner, he spends whole days out on the mountains reading Virgil and watching the stars. His painted horizons are lofty, with strong, deep blues; his reds have an extraordinary resonance.' He goes on to observe that Cézanne's backgrounds are as realistic as they are imaginative, that his paintings are completely original and that the Master of Aix is as mystical as his own drawing. It is worth adding that Gauguin made use of certain stylistic elements from Cézanne's work; in many still-lifes, even ones dating from

12

his last years, the memory of Cézanne is still sharp and clear. Gauguin's relationship with Pissarro continued until 1886, in the Breton landscapes and in particular in the Pont-Aven series. But other influences were beginning to crowd in on him. His ideas were being confirmed by physical and emotional sensations. The voyage · to Martinique satisfied all the dreams he had held during his earlier long sea voyages; the visits to Brittany in 1888 and 1889 laid the foundations of a new vision, which was to be matured and developed in Tahiti from 1891 to 1893. By now his impressionist vision was giving way to a kind of probing into the mysterious kernel of the human mind. He could see clearly into his own mind, and now began to depart from subjection to an object painted from real life, outlining his paintings directly from his inner consciousness. He went so far as to advise his friend Schuffenecker not to paint from life, because art ' is an abstraction which is accomplished by dreaming amid natural surroundings. '

The tropical vegetation of Martinique, the empty beaches, the violence of the Ocean, the native inhabitants, the harsh colours and the brilliance of the light were all to be brought together later in paintings composed of broad patches of colour; this synthesis is very different from the minute variations of shade in the *Willows* painted primarily under the influence of Pissarro.

The inspiration gained from his exotic voyage is the keynote of his Breton paintings; these tend, in the words of Albert Aurier, to be ' completely flat surfaces on which decorative patches of colour are juxtaposed '. The idea of decoration can be defined in terms of mural painting; Aurier saw Gauguin's painting as specifically intended for indoor or outdoor walls, directed as it was to formal ' primitive ' simplification, reaching ' beyond the horses of the Parthenon to the wooden horses that children play with. ' This was the start of Gauguin's journey towards the origins of mankind, a first essay in his flight to the ' Barbary that renews ones youth '. This mythical place differed from the barbary of Polynesian idols, and might be identified with the crude sincerity and rough innocence of the Breton calvaries and crucifixes.

' I love Brittany ', said Gauguin in 1888. ' When I walk along in my sabots on the granite earth I hear the hollow, powerful sound that I am looking for in my painting. ' It would be difficult to find better words to express the intensity of Gauguin's emotion than these. Expressed in pictorial terms it resulted in ' syntheticism ', based on pure colour, ' the passionate equivalent of a sensation ', which in its turn resulted in the school of Pont-Aven, with Gauguin as its leader.

The fundamental doctrine of the school of Pont-Aven was ' to exalt colour and to simplify form '. The painting which interprets this doctrine best is *The Vision after the Sermon, or Jacob wrestling with the Angel* (1888, *pl. 12*). The figures of Breton women in white bonnets in the foreground gave Emile Bernard occasion to accuse his master, whom he had always seemed to regard with undying admiration, of plagiarism. Bernard had painted a picture of *Breton Women in a Field* (with the same white bonnets) before Gauguin and he therefore considered himself as a precursor of the syntheticist movement. In fact the white bonnets were traditional dress and might have inspired anybody. The most cursory comparison of the two paintings shows that Bernard's was only a careful reproduction of traditional manners and dress, whereas Gauguin's *Vision* is planned on a scheme reminiscent of Lautrec's *At Fernando's Circus* and the two wrestlers recall a woodcut by Hokusai. It is a daring and prophetic representation of an imaginary world laden with symbolism, upon which modern art, from the Nabis and fauves to the expressionists, was to draw heavily.

Emile Bernard had introduced Paul Sérusier to Gauguin in 1888, in Mère Gloanec's inn in Pont-Aven, and Sérusier, more of a philosopher than a painter, had introduced him in his turn to Maurice Denis. This was the beginning of a series of encounters with younger artists who moved in symbolist circles, with innovators who had moved away from meteorological impressionism and the careful study of the time of day and the weather. Japanese prints were interpreted in a way which differed from that of Manet or Monet. They were appreciated in the same free spirit which

14

led to the discovery of Epinal prints and sign painting (it was not important that Gauguin, as we shall later discover, was susceptible to the classicism of Puvis de Chavannes, the Poussin of the Third Republic, and was spoken of, as were Van Gogh and Cézanne, as an artist turned 'towards a new classical order ').

Maurice Denis clearly perceived the significance of this exploitation of new sources of inspiration in popular and exotic art; it was this that gave symbolism its anti-classical and anti-rationalistic character. In 1917 Denis wrote that the most important aspect of symbolism was its attitude to nature. Nature should be represented, not reproduced. How? With plastic and painted equivalents.

Sérusier, who had shown Denis (like a letter of introduction) the lid of a cigar box, painted by Gauguin in bright, clear colours, recalled that the painter remarked: 'The tree is green. All right, paint it with the most beautiful green on your palette'. And on another occasion: 'Colours are the colours in the tubes of paint, not the colours of nature. If you see a shadow which looks slightly blue, go ahead and paint it with the brightest blue that you have.' This was a straightforward and decisive way of painting with patches of pure colour, a revolutionary method which admitted no half measures. Sérusier observed on this subject that '. . . (Gauguin) was fiercely individualistic and yet was bound to the most anonymous popular traditions.' Then: 'We supplemented Gauguin's basic teaching, substituting for his too simple theory of pure colour the theory of harmony infinitely varied as in nature.'

A further element in his vocabulary was the blue border round every shape, called *cloisonnisme*, derived from Japanese prints and medieval stained glass windows, and which was used felicitously in the early years of the twentieth century, particularly by the Italian Gino Rossi.

Gauguin, in the course of his careful meditations about art, had arrived at the conclusion that ' grey does not exist. Each object has its form and colour clearly outlined by a border.' In a letter to Schuffenecker on 14 January 1885 Gauguin seems to have anticipated theoretical symbolism – moments of illumination alternating with periods of doubt, negation and discomfort. There are moments when he should 'conserve his moral energy by closing the doors of his heart'; he declared to his wife that 'the duty of an artist is to work and become strong', and with proud self-confidence to be a great artist. His confidence in being a great artist was never shaken, and this made it possible for him to react in his paintings against fate, which was so often against him. His reaction against circumstances gave him his reputation as a strong man, as a man who had won the 'right to do what he liked'. He stood out from his contemporaries because of his very original way of looking at things, and his personality, which was capable of resolving the most disparate collection of cultural tit-bits into a unified whole. The most painstaking modern criticism (in particular by Field and Dorival) has been successful in sorting out masses of documents and dates, often enough taken directly from papers found on Hiva Oa after Gauguin's death by Victor Segalen, or in the archives of Monfreid's heirs.

The question of plagiarism was raised after Bernard's accusations on the subject of the *Vision after the Sermon*. A list of sources from which Gauguin took much of his inspiration would be far too long to include here. For my purposes it will suffice to reduce the very complex material to a simple outline.

Dorival, in an essay published in *The Burlington Magazine* (1951), has analysed 'Les Sources de l'Art de Gauguin provenant de Java, l'Egypte et de la Grèce Ancienne'; these include the bas-reliefs from the Temple of Baraboudour, an Egyptian bas-relief in the Louvre and some of the *metopes* from the Parthenon. The list continues with Delacroix, Prud'hon, Tassaert, Merino (a little-known Peruvian painter represented in the Arosa collection) for the *Riders on the Beach* (*pls 80-1*); an illustration called *The Apple Woman* by someone called Gray, published in *Le Courrier Français* (1844 and 1845), Chaplin, Millet, Daumier, Courbet, Degas, Manet (Gauguin made a copy of his *Olympia*), Pissarro, Cézanne, Lautrec, Redon, Puvis de Chevannes. In 1899 Gauguin wrote to Fontaines: ' Puvis overwhelms one with talent and experience... You gave me great pleasure when you admitted having thought (mistakenly) that my compositions (like the composition of Puvis de Chavannes) were based on an abstract idea which I was trying to make concrete by representing it in paint.' In 1901 he wrote to Charles Morice: 'Puvis explains his idea, yes, but he doesn't paint it. He is Greek, whereas I am a savage, a wolf of the forest without a collar. Puvis would entitle a painting *Purity* and, to explain the title, would paint a young virgin with a lily in her hand – a well-known symbol, understood by everybody. Gauguin, under the title *Purity*, will paint a landscape with limpid waters and unsullied by civilized man. Perhaps one figure. Without going into detail: there is a whole world between me and Puvis.'

The list continues with *Primavera* and the *Birth of Venus* by Botticelli, a 'Crucifix' at Trémalo and a 'Calvary' in Nizon, medieval stained glass windows, Japanese prints by Utamaro, Hokusai and Kuniyoshi and Tahitian native art. Field's additions are interesting: a piece of sculpture from the Theatre of Dionysus in Athens, the *Bath* and *Joseph with Potiphar's Wife* by Prud'hon, objects from the Marquesas Islands, an idol from New Zealand, a drawing of the school of Rembrandt, Van Gogh, *The Dying Horseman and the Devil* by Dürer, figures by Delacroix, a Tahitian photograph dating from about 1880 of a magpie drinking at a spring and, last but not least, Emile Bernard.

From all the examples quoted and documented by Field and Dorival one could piece together the strangest, most complex mosaic – composed of Gauguin's barefaced 'thefts', as often as not from photographs which (as we learn from a letter to Redon) he had taken with him to Tahiti and to his last home in Hiva Oa.

So was Gauguin a large-scale plagiarist? A possible reply to that is that he never improvised; he made lengthy studies, both drawings and watercolours, for his compositions and during the stages of elaboration would insert (one only needs to look at the final sketch of the great painting *Where do we come from? What are we? Where are we going?*, a forest of symbols and figures drawn from the most varied sources) an Indonesian sculpture, a drawing of the School of Rembrandt or a fragment of Courbet. But he was not really aiming at a 'savage' interpretation of the women in the Egyptian bas-relief in the Louvre in his *The Market* (*pls 48-9*). Everything that he assimilated in this way was to become a vital part of the composition of a painting; his borrowings never appeared as mere appendages, upsetting the balance of a work. The Crucifix at Trémalo was transformed into the *Yellow Christ* (*pl. 23*); the *Apple Woman* from the *Courrier Français* became *Tahitian Women with Mango Blossoms*; Bernard's traditional white bonnets were transposed through Gauguin's imagination into the women watching Jacob struggling with the angel on the red Breton earth; Botticelli's *Venus* assumes the shape of a Tahitian Venus in *Pape Pape Nace*. In each of these cases the original painting has been superseded or done away with; the new composition bears the unmistakeable mark of Gauguin's personality.

Historical research into his sources is still useful as it enables us to follow the creative process through every unforeseeable development. It is interesting to be able to establish what relationship Gauguin had with his contemporaries (apart from his borrowings from their work). First and foremost with Van Gogh, then with Degas, Redon, Puvis de Chavannes, and of course with the younger artists who admired him, such as Sérusier, Séguin, Laval, de Haan, Filinger, the group at Le Pouldu and the painters who shared his exhibition at the Café Volpini in 1889: Schuffenecker, Fauché, Anquetin, Daniel de Monfreid, Roy, Bernard.

Gauguin's first meeting with Van Gogh took place in Arles in October 1888. The two men were too different ever to get on together. After only a few days their discussions were becoming arguments. The brotherhood they had hoped for proved not to be possible. Van Gogh painted impulsively, urged forward by a feverish need to express himself; Gauguin left little to chance and hated improvisation. Van Gogh admired Monticelli, Ziem, Daubigny, Théodore Rousseau. Gauguin preferred Raphael, Ingres and Degas. Before setting off for Arles, Gauguin had sent Vincent his self-portrait. As soon as he saw it Van Gogh said: 'A prisoner without a ray of gaiety'. Gauguin however had written to Schuffenecker about it in these terms: 'I think it is one of my best paintings: so abstract as to be absolutely incomprehensible.' On first sight it looks like the head of a criminal, a Jean Valjean (the hero of Hugo's *Les Misérables*) impersonating an impressionist painter; travelling the world lugging his ball and chain with him. The drawing of it is completely original and certainly very abstract. The eyes, mouth and nose are symbols like the flowers on a Persian carpet. The colours differ a good deal from natural colours, vaguely recalling the colours of pottery fired at a high temperature. The brilliant reds and purples are streaked with blazing sparks like a fiery furnace: the furnace of Gauguin's mind. The background is chrome yellow with tiny naif bunches of flowers scattered over it. Like a child's bedroom wallpaper. When Gauguin later painted Van Gogh's portrait with a bunch of sunflowers, Van Gogh said: 'Yes, that's me all right, but mad.'

Apart from these differences their views of Arles and the surrounding countryside were completely opposite. Van Gogh saw everything in the colours of Daumier; Gauguin was reminded of something by Puvis: very brightly coloured and with something in common with Japanese painting. 'Van Gogh is a romantic', Gauguin said, 'and I have a tendency towards primitivism'. 'His Negro women are wonderfully expressive', Van Gogh declared when he saw some paintings of Martinique.

Provence was very different from Brittany; it had neither 'the stout, strong buildings, nor the spirituality, nor the emotive sadness'. Nevertheless Gauguin recognized Provence as 'the source of an admirable modern style', which had nothing in common with Seurat's hated '*petit-point*'. It is interesting to examine the way Van Gogh made it clear to Gauguin what subjects he preferred, making his famous models pose together in the café at night; the postman Roulin, the Zouave, Madame Ginoux. Gauguin did a quick sketch of Madame Ginoux and Van Gogh used it for the various different versions he made of *L'Arlésienne*. The painters worked together in the courtyard of the hospital as well as in the café, painting the same pair of old women. Their two interpretations give some idea, with conclusive visible evidence, of their two personalities, each trying to express their private world of emotion and feelings. In different letters Van Gogh wrote 'The arrival of Gauguin in Arles will change my painting significantly' and 'I owe a lot to Gauguin'. Gauguin himself viewed the situation less unselfishly. His total egoism was particularly thrown into relief at the time of Van Gogh's tragic death. Vincent's brother Théo van Gogh was struck by apoplexy immediately after his brother's death, and Gauguin, in a letter to Bernard, advised against the organization of a Van Gogh exhibition on the pretext that it would be wrong to draw attention to his madness just when his brother had gone mad as well. 'Too many people say our painting is lunacy. We should risk damaging our own reputations, without doing Vincent any good.' Gauguin's preoccupation with his own reputation contrasts with Van Gogh's generosity; in a letter to Aurier a few months before his death he had written: 'Your article [in the *Mercure de France*] would have been more accurate and, I think, more influential if, when you talked about the future of "tropical painting" and the problem of colour, you had discussed Gauguin at length before mentioning me'.

Gauguin had behaved just as ungenerously to Degas, to whom he owed a lot both as a painter and as a person. The tremendous compositional freedom in most of Degas' paintings reminds one of the action of a mechanical excavator, wresting the last atom of meaning from an expression or a gesture. Gauguin had borrowed from his paintings more than once during his years in Brittany, up to 1889. Besides, Degas had been one of the few faithful buyers at the sales organized at the Hôtel Drouot before Gauguin's first and second trips to Tahiti. In spite of this, Gauguin wrote to Bernard in 1889: 'Degas is growing old and is furious at not having found *le dernier mot*'.

Gauguin's relationship with Redon is less easy to pin-point, although Dorival puts forward certain exact references in paintings from the Tahitian period: there are links in the drawing, and in particular in the use of colour, so different from that of the impressionists; Gauguin's use of chiaroscuro, like that of Redon, creates 'a curious spiritual climate, full of sadness and mystery'. Besides this, still according to Dorival, they are connected by their surrealist tendency, their 'certainty that reality is not confined to the outward appearance of things', their 'sense of mystery'. Redon was a more shadowy character, far more secretive than Gauguin and possessed of a delicate artistic sense, a hermit who abandoned himself to fantastic dreams, permeated by symbolist literature, yet with an almost magical influence, an intellectual, reserved and enclosed in his aristocratic detachment. In spite of the differences of their characters, Gauguin and he held each other in esteem and affection, possibly in deference to their shared scorn of the scientific pretensions of the impressionists and pointillists and their common faith in the importance of dreams.

Puvis de Chavannes carried the classical ideal forward to the end of the century with a strange revival of Renaissance forms. Like the Pre-Raphaelites, Puvis painted imaginary scenes from bygone days. But in place of Dante Gabriel Rossetti's dreams, or Gustave Moreau's enigmatic, symbolic crowd scenes, Puvis chose rational composition, the forced immobility of sculptured figures, cerebral painting inspired by the great Italian masters of the fifteenth century and transformed by the matter-of-fact outlook of bourgeois society into ridicule of the myths of progress. Gauguin saw in Puvis something that he lacked and followed his example in compositions which came close to the Art Nouveau style, such as the *Poor Fisherman* (*pl. 66*), 1896, and *Nave Nave Mahama* (*pls 67-8*); his idea was to impose an all-over decorative scheme on his model. Perhaps Puvis does not deserve the oblivion into which he has passed; his paintings of the Sorbonne and the Parthenon, though they gave Gauguin the wrong idea about classicism, belong in the same category as the paintings of the Italian Sartorio; their intended symbolism far outweighs the artistic inventiveness displayed in them.

Maurice Denis, when he saw the first of the paintings Gauguin painted in Tahiti, rightly classified Gauguin as 'a Poussin without classical learning'. We should bear in mind, however, Gauguin's own words: 'My God, painting's difficult; how to express thought pictorially rather than in literary terms?'

The fascination which Gauguin's personality exercised on the young painters, who hung on his every word in Pont-Aven and Le Pouldu as if he were a prophet, is not really surprising, even though his opinions were dogmatically and obscurely expressed. Their relationship with him was a kind of collective collaboration, a continual exchange of ideas about nature and painting. Each person proffered his ideas, often enough fairly fragmentary, and the subject was elaborated; everyone took part, from Bernard to Sérusier (the philosopher of the group).

But in the eyes of contemporary society Gauguin, the leader, was a madman, the painter of red horses. The admirers he could rely on were very few, beginning with Maurice Denis who, in 1891, wrote to Sérusier: 'What are we waiting for to shout at the top of our voices, since otherwise no one will recognize the fact, that the painter of the *Yellow Christ, Jacob wrestling* and the bas-relief *Be in Love* is a genius, no less?'.

Gauguin replied indirectly to this enthusiasm (which was perfectly sincere) in a letter to Morice about his young followers: 'They are very clever... but perhaps they would exist without me? They would be accepted even if I didn't exist.' Other kindred spirits were few. Some of Albert Aurier's fundamental ideas about symbolism had been inspired by Gauguin, for example: 'The task of painting is to decorate the walls of buildings with thoughts, dreams and ideas.'

Le Pouldu had been a sort of 'French Tahiti' for Gauguin; now the ideas developed in Brittany were confirmed in the paintings he did in Tahiti. His journey to the islands completed his journey towards a dreamed-of concept of painting, already formed in his mind. The statuesque Maori women he met, standing quite still in poses which contradicted classical ideas of nobility (or the academic convention of the classic nude) excited his mind and his senses; he declared when he disembarked in Tahiti: 'Free at last, now I can love, sing and die.'

'The proportions of their bodies distinguish Maori women from all other women, and sometimes cause them to be mistaken for men. A Maori woman is like Diana the Huntress, but with broad shoulders and slim hips. However thin a woman's arm is the bones show very little; their figures are lissom and graceful. Their thighs are very strong but not stocky, and this makes them look very round... lastly their skin is a golden yellow.' This portrait is completed by the observation that their eyes meditate on dark dreams, gazing fixedly at the mystery of an 'unfathomable enigma'. At last the primitive world was yielding to his desire to discover it. The Eves of Tahiti were models uncorrupted by academic poses; nature offered new colours and new forms to stimulate the imagination of the artist, the light in which the tropical islands were bathed was that of some lost earthly paradise.

'Even before knowing what a picture represents... one is gripped by a magical harmony.' Gauguin paraphrased Denis' famous words referring to musical harmony. This idea recurs several times in the *Correspondence*, in particular when the colour of a certain kind of Tahitian interior is being described: the idea is clarified in a letter to André Fontainas of March 1899. 'You often go to the Louvre; next time you go remember what I say and look carefully at Cimabue. And remember at the same time the important part played by music in modern painting. The colours vibrate like musical notes, capturing that essence which is most widespread in nature and yet most difficult to catch: its interior energy.'

Gauguin's colours certainly vibrate in the Tahitian paintings; he uses broad patches of brilliant colour to render the intensity of the island light, the light brings the figures and landscapes to life and links everything together in subtle and peculiar relationships.

In an interview which he gave to the *Ecole de Paris* on 13 May 1895, Gauguin made his ideas even clearer: 'In my paintings every detail is carefully weighed and studied first of all. Just as in musical composition... To stimulate the imagination as music does, without recourse to ideas or pictures, but solely through that mysterious affinity which exists without a shadow of doubt between certain combinations of lines and colours and the mind of man.' He added sarcastically: 'Do you want to know what will be the most accurate form of art before long? Photography in colour, which will be with us shortly.' When his interviewer asked him why he did not want to be classified as revolutionary, Gauguin replied: 'It is a ridiculous term. Roujon first applied it to me. I told him that every artist whose work differs from that of his predecessors is worthy of the name revolutionary.'

Exotic painting should not be confused with folklore. For Gauguin exotic painting meant the possession of a mysterious image which had emanated from the earth, like the breath of some animal. Earth, he said, is our animal spirit. And when he wanted to get back to the primordial purity of life he spoke of joyful savages, unfettered freedom which increased his detachment from the bastard civilization of Europeans. 'My Eve is almost an animal. That is why she is chaste in spite of her nakedness, whereas all the Venuses in the Salon are indecent and immodest.' (See pl. 83.)

This man who wore only a brightly coloured loincloth (which must have betrayed the whiteness of this particular cannibal) had the eye of a civilized man, turned, more than he would have willingly believed, towards Paris. He claimed not to want praise or glory, but he anxiously awaited the judgment of his few distant friends on the canvases that he had sent, months beforehand, to France. The simple life did not really satisfy him; he was conscious of being worthy of the consideration and admiration of his successors.

And yet, between illnesses and excesses and difficulties of every nature, though he repeatedly said that he could not go on any longer, and had decided to give up his painting, he continued to paint in the most brave and brilliant colours; he portrayed, with symbols and representations, the myths and customs of Polynesian life, learnt from books or from everyday contacts with the natives whose life he shared.

Between 1897 and 1898, Gauguin entered his most acute crisis, which brought him to a dramatic suicide attempt. But from the brink of despair his pride led him back to his painting, and he began again with savage energy. In this state he painted *Where do we come from? What are we? Where are we going?*, which Jean Leymarie has called his spiritual testimony. This painting is nearly four metres long, and painted predominantly in blue and a sort of Veronese green; groups of figures are seated on either side of the central figure, a naked man picking a fruit from a tree, with his arms in the air. Gauguin ' put all his energy, all the mournful passion of the terrible state he was in, into this precise and scrupulous vision; anything that seems hurried disappears and makes way for the abundant life which springs from the painting. ' Gauguin was fascinated by his work; he described it to Monfreid in terms which convey it very clearly. He would stand looking at it for long periods and confessed to Monfreid that he admired it.

As has already been observed it is a long frieze showing symbolic figures, taken from a variety of sources, but ' the symbolism is sensual rather than intellectual '. Before we are even aware of it we take in the purity of the colours, which offer us a magical vision of an imaginary life; this picture expresses all that is most original in Gauguin's art, at the height of his artistic maturity. It is, in the profoundest sense of the term, his masterpiece. In it Gauguin has summed up his whole world of barbaric dreams; this is the climax of his search for primordial purity.

As Gauguin intended, the thing that fascinates one immediately about this painting, before any intellectual, critical methods are brought into use, is the all-over harmony of the theme, which impresses itself on the consciousness like the dominant theme of a symphony. To arrive at the intensity of feeling expressed here, Gauguin had sunk to the lower depths of moral and physical suffering. But this picture does not only represent a relief through art from his intolerable sufferings. Under the influence of his barbaric island his vision had grown more clear-cut and acute, and had attained freedom; his mind had transformed the South Seas into a setting for a poetic and mysterious myth.

Gauguin had made sculptured figures which might have been Polynesian idols; his Christ had the strength of a Romanesque carving; his wood-cuts had portrayed life in a savage, far-off land. In each of these media he had increased the scope of the grand poem in images which occupied his imagination. All his energy was channelled into the quest which he had conceived in Brittany and continued in Tahiti and Hiva Oa – the quest for an ideal art, almost a mystical experience, which would find its expression only in the furthest corner of a land untouched by civilization. This adventure came to its tragic end. But before its conclusion it had given birth to modern art. In June 1899, Gauguin wrote to Maurice Denis: 'The first part of my plan has born fruit; now you may do what you please and, what is most important, no one will be shocked.' Matisse for one took this important lesson to heart.

No one has expressed the real meaning of Gauguin's great adventure better than Henri Focillon: 'It is not by an artificial or literary effort that Gauguin finds his way to the shores of an immemorial past. He seems to have been there already, to have lived there for a long time and then to have come back to us from below, through the shadows and the days, holding in his hand an imperishable wooden god polished with an implement of stone.'

Gauguin and the Critics

The number of writings and contemporary documents which deal with the life and work of Gauguin is immense, but by far the most important among them are the letters and writings of the painter himself: *Lettres à Daniel de Monfreid* (new edition 1950); *Lettres à sa femme et à ses amis* (new ed. 1949); *Lettres à Emile Bernard* (1954); *Noa Noa* (new ed. 1966); *Avant et après; Racontars d'un rapin; Ancien culte Mahori; Cahiers pour Aline* (1897). A complete list of his letters would include many other unpublished ones, preserved in the archives of M. Luc de Monfreid.

News of his life and ideas about art are all jumbled together with dates and descriptions of Polynesian life, written in the direct style of a diary. Gauguin used to get down to his writing when his physical disabilities prevented him from painting. During his final, harrowing months between 1902 and 1903, in the isolation of Hiva Oa, he spent a good deal of his time writing, alternating memoirs and thoughts with daily angry letters to the island authorities. *Avant et après* reflects the state of mind he was in, rebellious, angry and violent – on the borders of madness. These are the outpourings of a man who will not admit defeat, although he realises that death is near, and who lets his pen run where his momentary whim leads it. There are some interesting passages, nevertheless, which, like some of the descriptions in *Noa Noa*, deserve to be regarded as a literary counterpart to his paintings, inspired by his sincere love of primitive life and by the earthly paradise which civilized man has destroyed. Gauguin aspired to the state of Rousseau's noble savage, living naturally and expressing himself freely: but what sacrifice and what pain it cost him.

Alongside the hostile and negative criticism which refused to see any real meaning in his art, Gauguin had favourable recognition from Huysmans and Mallarmé, Octave Mirbeau and Charles Morice, Gide and, with some reserve, Strindberg; also from the young critic Albert Aurier who wrote about him from 1891 onwards.

Letters from artists, from Van Gogh, Maurice Denis, and Paul Sérusier and from the faithful Schuffenecker and Daniel de Monfreid, all confirm to what extent Gauguin's ' savage ' vision was comprehended by the young, from his disciples at the School of Pont-Aven to the Nabis. Official circles on the other hand all reacted in the same way as the Director-General of the Beaux Arts, Roujon, who had declared to Charles Morice that he would keep Gauguin's work out of the national collections at all costs. Roujon was a typical member of that dyed-in-the-wool bureaucracy which, from Paris to Hiva Oa, was the enemy of the painter of red horses. This explains the destruction of so many paintings, left by Gauguin in Papeete and the Marquesas Islands, by zealous petty officials. There were other cases of destruction for more sinister motives – lack of comprehension or sheer jealousy. Pissarro, to whom Gauguin, whilst still a broker's agent, had turned as his master, and Emile Bernard, his first great admirer, both later turned against him. Pissarro was upset by Gauguin's slighting references to pointillism and Seurat's ' *petit-point* '. Bernard accused him of plagiarism in *Jacob wrestling with the Angel*, revealing the typical acrimony of a failed painter towards Gauguin. Although Van Gogh and Cézanne had both been close friends of his, and had regarded him as being full of promise, Bernard ended up in Cairo painting murals in churches and in Italy copying Renaissance paintings.

Many years were to pass between the day in 1903 when M. Fayet, who had paid a few hundred francs for the picture, sold *Ta Arii Vahine* (1896) for 30,000 francs and 25 November 1959 when *You are waiting for a Letter* was sold for £ 130,000 or 180 milion old francs.

Critical appreciation moves more slowly than the world market. In 1906 the Salon d'Automne presented the first big retrospective exhibition of Gauguin's works, and included 227 of his paintings. In the same year the first monograph on the artist was published, written by Jean de Rotonchamp. Charles Morice published his monograph in 1919, Robert Rey in 1924. Jean Dorsenne's study of Gauguin's relationship with his wife, Mette Gad, followed in 1927 and in the same year appeared Michel Guérin's study of his graphic work. A series of monographs followed: A. Alexandre (1930), A. Bertram (1930), B. Ternoviz (1934), R. Cogniat (1936), J. Rewald (1938), L. Hautecoeur (1942), M. Malingue (1944), R. Cogniat (1947).

The biographies which contain the most information, sometimes previously unpublished, are by Maurice Malingue (1948) and Henri Perruchot (1961). The memoir by Gauguin's son Pola, entitled *Gauguin, mon père*, is interesting. Also noteworthy is the catalogue of the Gauguin exhibition at the Orangerie in 1949, edited by Jean Leymarie with a preface by René Huyghe, *Gauguin créateur de la peinture moderne*, and Raymond Cogniat's volume entitled *La Vie ardente de Paul Gauguin*, with an interesting preface by Henri Focillon. The final passage of this preface is worth quoting as it contains a thought often disregarded by the critic keen to romanticize Gauguin's life: ' Gauguin's glory does not reside in his having added a chapter to the history of primitive curiosities, or some hitherto unpublished adventures to the collection of navigators' log-books and memoirs. It is time we stopped thinking of him as the hero of a seafaring story, one of Robert Louis Stevenson's more colourful characters. Gauguin is really the opposite of picturesque and romantic. '

Two recent publications: *Gauguin* (1961) with essays by Huyghe, d'Angélis, Dorival, Field, Malingue, Nourissier, Perruchot, Rheims and Roger-Marx, and *Gauguin* (1936) by Georges Boudaille represent the sum total of studies and discoveries about his life and work. Nevertheless the most important book on Gauguin to date is the catalogue of his paintings, completed by Georges Wildenstein before his death and published in 1964 by Raymond Cogniat. A second volume, which will include a biography of Gauguin and complete documentary material covering his life and his works, as well as a catalogue of prints, drawings, sculpture and pottery, is now being published under the editorship of Raymond Cogniat.

We owe to Wildenstein and Cogniat (and also to Malingue, Perruchot, Huyghe and Leymarie) an accurate reconstruction of Gauguin's life, freed from legendary accretions. Another important book was published in 1966: the authentic text of *Noa Noa*, thanks to the painstaking research of Jean Loïze, who has written a preface to the work, and added a series of unpublished documents, a life of the artist, exhaustive notes and a detailed bibliography which directs the reader to other available information.

Year by year, conscientious historical and critical studies have liberated Gauguin, just as Focillon recommended, from the accumulated accretions of romance and legend: they have brought him back from the land of myths into historical reality.

Notes on the Plates

1 The Seine at the Pont d'Iéna, 1875. Oil on canvas, 65×92 cm. Signed and dated. Paris, Jeu de Paume. Winter landscape painted from life, inspired by impressionism and particularly by Monet and Pissarro. Of Gauguin's early works this is perhaps the most interesting; he was very close to Guillaumin at the time, and really only regarded as a dilettante.

2 Study of a Nude, or Suzanne sewing, 1880. Oil on canvas, 115×80 cm. Signed and dated. Copenhagen, Ny Carlsberg Glyptotek. Painted five years after the previous picture. In the meantime Gauguin has gained confidence and energy in the painting of figures, departing from impressionist models. Huysmans praised this nude in 1881. Suzanne had been Delacroix' model, and Gauguin made a copy of his *Half-caste Girl* in 1878.

3 Snow in the Rue Carcel, 1883. Oil on canvas, 117×90 cm. Eva Kiaer collection, Copenhagen. The influence of Pissarro is very marked in this painting. It dates from a period when he and Gauguin had temporarily become firm friends. Pissarro was Gauguin's master, and made him exhibit his earliest works with the impressionists from 1879. This picture was painted from within the boundaries of impressionism.

4 The Road to the Village, 1884. Oil on canvas, 60×73 cm. Boston, Museum of Fine Arts. The choice of subject reflects Pissarro's influence. Gauguin studied the scene in great detail, conscientiously correcting and improving his vision.

5 Village Street, 1884. Oil on canvas, 55×46 cm. Signed and dated. Zurich, Hausammann collection.

6 Still-life with Mandoline, 1884. Oil on canvas, 64×53 cm. Signed and dated. Paris, Jeu de Paume. Painted during a year of intense hard work in Copenhagen, Dieppe and Paris, spent investigating the composition of still-lifes and culminating in the *Still-life with Horse's Head*.

7 Still-life with Horse's Head, 1885. Oil on canvas, 48×38 cm. Signed. Paris, private collection. Pissarro had been introduced to Georges Seurat by Paul Signac in Guillaumin's studio. Gauguin here uses an almost pointillist style, very unusual for him, most like that of Seurat; the light is systematically broken up into dots of all colours. There are no other examples of Gauguin's use of this style, either during this year or later.

8 On the Beach II, 1887. Oil on canvas, 46×61 cm. Signed and dated. Paris, private collection. The colour is applied in flat patches, outlined here and there by a dark border. This is the beginning of a new phase in Gauguin's painting, based on the 'syntheticist' theories of the Pont-Aven school, applied to the luminous landscape of Martinique.

9-10 Four Breton Women dancing, 1886. Oil on canvas, 72×91 cm. Signed and dated. Munich, Bayerische Staatsgemäldesammlungen. This is mentioned in a letter dated 1888 containing a list of pictures to be hung in the Café des Arts by Volpini. Painted in Brittany, with figures to be used again in other compositions. This is an early attempt at the 'syntheticist' style, which he developed more coherently in his paintings of Martinique.

11 Portrait of Madeleine Bernard, 1888. Oil on canvas, 72×58 cm. Signed and dated. Grenoble, Musée de Peinture et de Sculpture. Emile Bernard's sister Madeleine, aged seventeen, aroused Gauguin's curiosity and he soon fell in love with her. This painting shares certain qualities of *L'Arlésienne*, the maturity of its style and its originality which were to become pronounced in the Brittany paintings of 1889, after the tragic incident in Arles.

12 The Vision after the Sermon, or Jacob wrestling with the Angel, 1888. Oil on canvas, 73×92 cm. Signed and dated 1888. Edinburgh, National Gallery of Scotland. The figures of Jacob and the angel are inspired by a drawing by Hokusai; they and the Breton women with their white bonnets in the foreground seemed to Pissarro to indicate a return to Byzantium and to Japanese prints. He reproved Gauguin for 'not applying his syntheticism to modern philosophy, which is avowedly social, anti-authoritarian and anti-mystical'. Bernard's allegations of plagiarism do not detract in the slightest from the originality of Gauguin's painting. Albert Aurier thought of it as a fresco. It could also be an enlarged illumination from some imaginary Book of Hours painted in the syntheticist style, rather than the analytical style of Seurat. This is a painting of fundamental importance which opened all the doors to the artistic revolution of the early twentieth century.

13 At the Top of the Cliff, 1888. Oil on canvas, 75×60 cm. Signed and dated. Paris, Musée des Arts Décoratifs. The perspective of this view, seen from high up, transforms the scene into a series of blocks, a foretaste of the style of Gauguin's painting after his first trip to Tahiti.

14 The Garden of the Hospital, Arles, 1888. Oil on canvas, 73×92 cm. Signed and dated. Chicago, Art Institute. This shares the style of the *Vision after the Sermon*, and has the same feeling of being a fresco. The brilliance of the colours, painted in flat contrasting patches, also recalls Gothic stained glass.

15 Les Alyscamps, 1888. Oil on canvas, 92×73 cm. Signed and dated. Paris, Jeu de Paume. This romantic subject is bathed in the clear brilliance of Provençal light, yet without violent contrasts.

16 Peasants' Cottages, Arles, 1888. Oil on canvas, 72×92 cm. Signed and dated. Stockholm, Nationalmuseum. A brief period of calm during his difficult stay with Van Gogh. This painting was an isolated excursion into landscape painting in the sun-baked countryside of Provence.

17 La Belle Angèle, 1889. Oil on canvas, 92×73 cm. Signed and dated 1889. Paris, Jeu de Paume. Théo Van Gogh, in a letter to his brother, called this portrait 'fresh and pleasing' with something rustic about it, and he observed that the placing of the figure in a circle was inspired by Japanese art. This painting is reminiscent of an illuminated page as well, both in its layout and in the purity of the colours.

18 The Schuffenecker Family, 1889. Oil on canvas, 73×92 cm. Signed. Paris, Jeu de Paume. Schuffenecker had been a stockbroker with Gauguin, who regarded him as a conventional bourgeois, who was missing the life of freedom enjoyed by Gauguin. Nevertheless Schuffenecker came to his rescue time and again when he was in trouble. In this portrait the family is seen from an angle, a technique first adopted by Degas from photography. The camera had taught people to 'see' in a way entirely different from the traditional way.

19-20 Nirvana, Portrait of Meyer de Haan, 1889. Oil and turpentine on silk, 20×29 cm. Signed. Hartford, Conn., Wadsworth Atheneum. This is very close to the *Self-portrait with Yellow Christ*, both in the placing of the figures and in the background. Meyer de Haan was a Dutch painter who had worked with Gauguin at Le Pouldu. Here he is transformed into a diabolical character.

21 Self-portrait with Yellow Christ, 1889. Oil on canvas, 38×46 cm. Paris, private collection. The vitality of the self-portrait and the strong contrast of colour between the figure and the background combine to give a strong impression of fantasy. Gauguin portrays himself in the flower of almost brutal manhood.

22 Good Morning, Monsieur Gauguin, 1889. Oil on canvas, 113×92 cm. Signed and dated. Prague, Muzea moderniho umeni. During this intensely creative period, Gauguin continued to make discoveries about the rough, primitive countryside of Brittany, in the spirit of the *Vision after the Sermon*. Against a desolate winter landscape, leafless trees stand out in their nakedness. The atmosphere created by Gauguin has a dramatic power which was to influence the fauves and the expressionists. Even Gino Rossi, twenty years later, saw Brittany through Gauguin's eyes.

23 Yellow Christ, 1889. Oil on canvas, 92×73 cm. Signed and dated. Buffalo, Albright Art Gallery. The cross in the front of this painting divides it up into two open spaces, each with sky above a hilly landscape with splashes of trees with red leaves, and in the foreground a field in which three Breton women are sitting in meditative attitudes. The model for the figure of Christ was a wooden crucifix at Trémalo, now in the church at Nizon, a Romanesque medieval carving, naked and crude. *Yellow Christ* is the prototype for subsequent German painting, from ' Die Brücke ' to ' Der Blaue Reiter '.

24   Green Christ, or Breton Calvary, 1889. Oil on canvas, 92×73 cm. Signed and dated. Brussels, Musées Royaux des Beaux Arts. Inspired by the ' calvary ' at Nizon, near Pont-Aven, a sombre Romanesque carving in black granite. On a slip of paper which he gave to Albert Aurier, Gauguin wrote: ' Calvary / cold stone / from the Breton earth-soul / of the sculpture who reveals, / religion through his Breton soul / in Breton dress and / local colour and / a passive Breton ram. ' The monumental group of figures is seen against a wild background of cliffs, beaten by the angry Atlantic breakers, a true representation of the ' earth-soul ' of ancient Brittany.

25-6   Still-life with Fan, 1889. Oil on canvas, 30×61 cm. 1889. Paris, Jeu de Paume. The fruit, fan and assorted objects crop up more than once in different arrangements, in still-lifes painted at Le Pouldu, under the influence of Cézanne.

27   Children at Le Pouldu, 1889. Oil on canvas, 93×74 cm. Unterwald, Switzerland, collection of Mme Alf. Schienle Hergiswil. The bashful Breton children in their picturesque costumes were favourite models of Gauguin, who was looking for exotic local colour among the peasants before setting off again towards a land of his dreams.

28   The Gate, 1889. Oil on canvas, 92×73 cm. Signed and dated. Zurich, Alfred Hausammann collection. The old gate may be the same as the one in *Good Morning, Monsieur Gauguin*. Here it is in the foreground, in sharp relief, and contrasts significantly with the landscape behind, where the influence of Gauguin's trip to Martinique is already in evidence.

29-30   Blue Roof, or Farmhouse at Le Pouldu, 1890. Oil on canvas, 73×92 cm. Signed and dated. Emery Reves collection. Meyer de Haan also painted this subject. Gauguin had by this time become an influential member of the circle of painters working at Le Pouldu. His mysterious personality and the audacity of his ideas, proclaimed sometimes with passionate rhetoric, sometimes with cold logic, combined to give him this power. Many paintings of this period, by Laval, Sérusier, and Meyer de Haan, were later attributed to Gauguin.

31   Portrait of a Woman with a Still-life by Cézanne, 1890. Oil on canvas, 65×55 cm. Signed and dated. Chicago, Art Institute. Cézanne's still-life, painted in the background, belonged to Gauguin (no. 341 in Lionello Venturi's *Catalogo di Cézanne*). The same painting was reproduced by Maurice Denis in his famous *Homage to*

Cézanne. Gauguin's admiration for the master of Aix is made very clear in this portrait of Marie Derrien.

32 The Loss of Virginity, or The Re-awakening of Spring, 1891. Oil on canvas, 90×130 cm. Provincetown, Mass., Chrysler Art Museum. Leymarie drew attention to the 'demoniacal and sexual' nature of this painting, a portrait of Juliette Huet, Gauguin's mistress (she died, very old, in 1935, 'having destroyed all letters and mementos of the painter'). It reflects Gauguin's predisposition for symbols and allegory, often from literary sources.

33 Self-portrait with Palette, 1891. Oil on canvas, 55×45 cm. Signed, with a dedication. New York, Arthur Sachs collection. Gauguin painted this from a photograph, dating probably from 1880, which was owned by Mme Jeanne Schuffenecker; he made additions and corrections.

34 Self-portrait with Idol, 1891. Oil on panel, 46×33 cm. Signed. San Antonio, Texas, Marion Koogler McNay Art Institute. The Oceanic idol in the background introduces a new concept to the enigmatic figure of the painting, with his thoughtful gaze and his air of being a *conquistador.*

35 Fantasy, or The Woman in a Red Dress, 1891. Oil on canvas, 92×73 cm. Signed and dated. Kansas City, William Rockhill Nelson Gallery of Art. The red of the woman's dress dominates the painting, which is visually close to the bourgeois 'intimist' style. The painting hanging on the wall is clearly by Gauguin, but curiously enough it is unknown.

36 Man with Axe, 1891. Oil on canvas, 92×70 cm. Signed and dated. New York, Alex M. Lewit collection. Gauguin's painting has by now been reduced to the straightforward scheme of a primitive mural. The change which had begun to work on him in Martinique was completed in Tahiti.

37-8 Two Women on the Beach, 1891. Oil on canvas, 69×91 cm. Signed and dated. Paris, Jeu de Paume. The two figures completely fill the yellow patch of beach and the deep emerald patch of sea; they stand solemnly, in simple positions, red and purple motifs.

39 Te Aa no Areois, 1891. Oil on canvas, 92×73 cm. Signed and dated. New York, Mrs William S. Paley collection. This is reminiscent of Puvis de Chavanne's *Hope,* translated into the Tahitian idiom. Puvis, the decorator of the Panthéon in Paris, was often quoted in syntheticist circles.

40 Nafea Foa Ipoipo (When shall we be married?), 1892. Oil on canvas, 105×77 cm. Signed and dated. Basle, Kunstmuseum. The figures are painted with almost no modelling, in brilliant colours. The sparkling landscape is very simply drawn. The group is like a group of sculptured figures, composed with a freedom which was unusual in paintings of the time; the apparently unmixed reds and yellows bring it to life.

41-2 Manao Tupapao (The spirit of the dead keeps watch), 1892. Oil on canvas, 73×92 cm. Signed and dated. U.S.A., collection of General Anson Gonger Goodyear. In a letter to his wife Gauguin tells her that he painted a nude portrait of a girl lying down in a dark and melancholy atmosphere, terrified by the spirit of the dead. Tehura dares not look at the spectres and will-o-the-wisps, as she is overcome by the terrors and superstitions of her race. Gauguin was convinced that he had painted a marvellous picture. And he was right.

43 Two Tahitian Women on the Beach, 1892. Oil on canvas, 91×64 cm. Honolulu, Hawaii, Academy of Arts. The beach, the sea, his solid, nude women (like the Venus in *La Terre Délicieuse*), figures which look as if they were carved out of wood like Polynesian idols. This is the natural and primevally innocent world which Gauguin dreamed of, far from the petty officials and vicious gendarmes of Papeete.

44 Tahitian Women on the Beach, 1892. Oil on canvas, 110×89 cm. Signed and dated. New York, Robert Lehmann collection. The atmosphere in this painting is very like the atmosphere of *Man with Axe*, especially the decorative linear rhythms and the bright patches of colour. It is a Matisse *avant la lettre*.

45-6 Fatata te miti (By the Sea), 1892. Oil on canvas, 68×92 cm. Signed and dated. Washington, D. C., National Gallery of Art. Here the painting creates its own myth; it is a mythical interpretation of reality. The fugitive image is captured in the realm of poetry, like a fable immortalized by music and colour, with mystical harmonies from the Orient. Art Nouveau has almost arrived. But Gauguin's magical symbolism has already transcended the style it helped to create.

47 Te Poipoi (Morning), 1892. Oil on canvas, 68×92 cm. Signed and dated. New York, Charles S. Payson collection. Le Pouldu had been a kind of French Tahiti for Gauguin. The images of an exotic landscape were already at work in his mind: he was only waiting to catch a glimpse of the distant lands to transform his mind's images into paintings. How this was done can be seen by comparing this Tahitian landscape with the Breton landscapes of 1889-90.

48-9 Ta Matete (The Market), 1892. Tempera on canvas, 73×92 cm. Signed and dated. Basle, Kunstmuseum. Gauguin took the composition of this frieze from a photograph of an Egyptian bas-relief in the British Museum. The repetition of the stylized gestures of the five women makes them like figures in a tapestry. They are sitting on a bench against a background rather like a stage set.

50-1 Areanea (Games), 1892. Oil on canvas, 75×94 cm. Signed and dated. Paris, Jeu de Paume. Another painting in the style of a mural. Thanks to the abstraction of the style a scene from everyday life assumes the aspect of a primitive fable. In a letter to Daniel de Monfreid, Gauguin remarked that even the pure colours he used did not succeed in giving his paintings final brilliance. He was referring to *Tahitian Pastoral*, in which the colours are particularly intense. He compared it, rather strangely, with ' an old Dutch master ' or a faded old tapestry.

52 Mahana Maa, 1892. Oil on canvas, 45×31 cm. Signed and dated. Helsinki, Atheneum. This represents the day when the weekly provisions are bought.

53 Matamua (Once upon a time), 1892. Oil on canvas, 93×72 cm. Signed and dated. New York, private collection. A synthesis of easily identifiable elements from different works, but one of the most characteristic of Gauguin's Tahitian paintings.

54-5 Otahi (Alone), 1893. Oil on canvas, 50×73 cm. Signed and dated. Paris, private collection. One of Gauguin's most sculptural figures, in a posture characteristic of the native women.

56 Hiha Tefaton (The Moon and the Earth), 1893. Oil on canvas, 112×62 cm. Signed and dated. New York, Museum of Modern Art. The same theme as in *Pape Moe*. The mysterious spring is taken from a famous photograph showing a young girl drinking water which is flowing from a rock. This painting illustrates an ancient Maori legend.

57 Ea Haere Ia Oe (Where are you going?), II, 1893. Oil on canvas, 91×71 cm. Signed and dated. Leningrad, Hermitage. This is a return to a theme treated in 1892, with the difference that the woman in the foreground now holds a mango, and that her sarong is pink with yellow patterns, almost as in a Matisse. On the other hand, the two women in front of the screen in the background are the same as in the earlier painting. Gauguin frequently took over elements from his own previous works in this way, adapting them to the needs of his new conception.

58-9 Mahana no Atua (Day of God), 1894. Oil on canvas, 70×91 cm. Signed and dated. Chicago, Art Institute. This painting unites many different elements taken from other works.

60 Village under Snow, 1894. Oil on canvas, 65×90 cm. Paris, Jeu de Paume. This was found, after Gauguin's death, on the easel in his studio and was thought to be his last painting. However an examination of the pigment and a careful historical investigation has shown that it probably dates from 1894, when Gauguin returned to Brittany.

61 The Siesta, 1894. Oil on canvas, 87×116 cm. New York, Ira Haupt collection. Gestures and movements which have been used previously are repeated here, in a decorative scheme which recalls Japanese art.

62 The Mill, 1894. Oil on canvas, 73×92 cm. Signed and dated. Paris, Jeu de Paume. The Moulin David at Pont-Aven. The Breton landscape is seen through changed eyes, since Gauguin's journey to Tahiti.

63-4 Te Tamari no Atua (The Birth of Christ, Son of God), 1896. Oil on canvas, 96×128 cm. Signed and dated. Munich, Bayerische Staatsgemäldesammlungen. In the background are two paintings by Gauguin. The right hand one after a *Stable* by Tussaert. The dense, erotic half-light captured Gauguin's imagination.

65 Self-portrait (at Golgotha), 1896. Oil on canvas, 76×64 cm. Signed and dated. São Paulo, Brazil, Museu de Arte. Gauguin's ' Peruvian ' profile seems to be less accentuated in this weary and painful self-portrait.

66 The Poor Fisherman, 1896. Oil on canvas, 76×66 cm. Signed and dated. São Paulo, Brazil, Museu de Arte. This was sent to Vollard in December 1896. The figure of the fisherman was repeated in the *Canoe*, now in Leningrad, painted in the same year.

67-8 Nave Nave Mahana (Wonderful Days), 1896. Oil on canvas, 94×130 cm. Signed and dated. Lyons, Musée des Beaux-Arts. The layout seems to come from Puvis de Chavannes. The colour is darker, as if dimmed by age. The decorations look forward to the linear style of Art Nouveau.

69-70 Nevermore, 1897. Oil on canvas, 68×116 cm. With the title. Signed and dated. London, Courtauld Institute of Art. The dominant colour is the yellow of the cushion supporting the girl's head, the same yellow as in *Te Tamari no Atua*. The element of symbolism does not match the naturalism of the nude figure very well. Is the background symbolic or not? Gauguin said that the title was not inspired by Poe's *Raven*; the raven had nothing to do with it. The bird is the devil's bird lying in wait. The man who yearned for silence, who wanted to be left in peace to die, forgotten by everybody, was in fact painting his greatest work; he justifies it in *Noa Noa* when he says: ' My God, painting's difficult; how to express thoughts pictorially rather than in literary terms? ' His pictorial means have been decried by his modern detractors, but Matisse admired them very deeply.

71 Te Rerioa (The Dream), 1897. Oil on canvas, 95×132 cm. Signed and dated. London, Courtauld Institute of Art. The two motionless women are squatting like two Buddhas, gazing dreamily into space. Gauguin interprets their mysterious dreams against a background of sculptured panels, in the dim indoor light of evening.

72-3 Vairumati, 1897. Oil on canvas, 73×94 cm. Signed and dated. Paris, Jeu de Paume. Gauguin described this girl, leaning diagonally on one hand, in *Noa Noa*: ' She was tall, and the fire of the sun's rays burned in the gold of her skin; all the mysteries of love breathed in the black night of her hair '. The tone of voice is somewhat baroque, but this picture confirms what he said.

74 The White Horse, 1898. Oil on canvas, 114×91 cm. Signed and dated. Paris, Jeu de Paume. This pastoral scene again forecasts Art Nouveau and the decorated *fin de siècle* stained glass. Jean Leymarie was reminded of a meaningful phrase from Mallarmé: ' It is extraordinary that so much mystery could be couched in so much brilliance. '

75 Still-life with ' L'Espérance ', 1901. Oil on canvas, 65×77 cm. Signed and dated. Chicago, Nathan Cummings collection. The sunflowers turn, this time on a table, and in the background is the photograph of a study by Puvis de Chavannes for *L'Allégorie de L'Espérance*. Gauguin for once abandons the exotic and uses a European scene.

76-7 And the Gold of their Bodies, 1901. Oil on canvas, 67×76 cm. Signed and dated. Paris, Jeu de Paume. This painting is inspired by a photograph of the frescoes in the Temple of Baraboudour, Java, which was later discovered by Segalen in Gauguin's studio. In his imaginative compositions Gauguin would use anything that struck his fancy, almost to the point of plagiarism. But his own personality was strong enough to transform things entirely.

78 Flowers in a Cup, 1901. Oil on canvas, 29×46. Signed. Chicago, Nathan Cummings collection. Cézanne and Chardin assailed the memory of the hermit of Hiva Oa in his distant corner of the world. Far from his native land and its traditions, he returns to their characteristic type of still-life.

79 Girl in Peignoir, 1902. Oil on canvas, 92×73 cm. Signed and dated. Essen, Museum Folkwang. The colouring is delicate with whites and greys, yellow ochres, dull pink and terracotta on a very light background with crimson streaks; the composition was drawn from a photograph taken inside Gauguin's house.

80-1 Riders on the Beach, 1902. Oil on canvas, 66×76 cm. Signed and dated. Essen, Museum Folkwang. The figures of the riders are painted with a primitive liberty, in accordance with Gauguin's policy of rebellion against convention. ' Nature must be represented with plastic and coloristic equivalents, not reproduced ' were Gauguin's words. ' If you see a blue shadow, you should paint it as blue as you possibly can. '

82 Nude Woman, 1900. Sculpture in wood. One of the most typical of Gauguin's carvings, inspired by Polynesian idols; this type of sculpture was to be taken up a few years later by Picasso and the cubists.

83 Tahitian Eve, 1891. Watercolour. Grenoble, Musée de Peinture et de Sculpture. A typical watercolour, taken from a painting in oils; one of the many illustrations for Gauguin's writings in which the drawing and colours were linked to the text; the relationship between text and drawings was very exactly worked out.

84-5 The Offering, 1892. Oil on canvas, 68×78 cm. Signed and dated. Zurich, Emil G. Bührle collection. A strong composition with two heavy figures in the foreground, painted against a delicate land-scape which has all the freshness of spring.

1

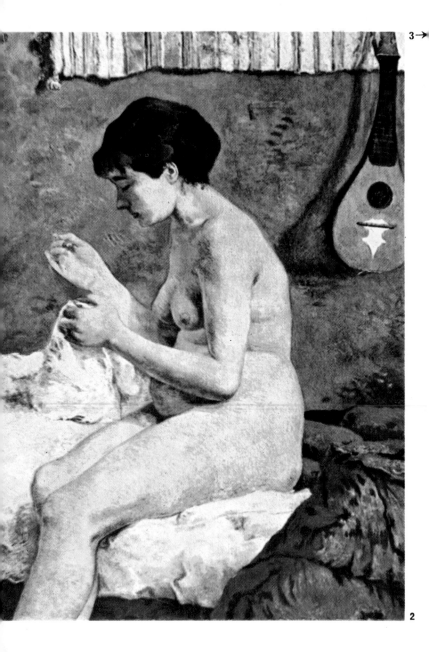

8

9

12 –

11

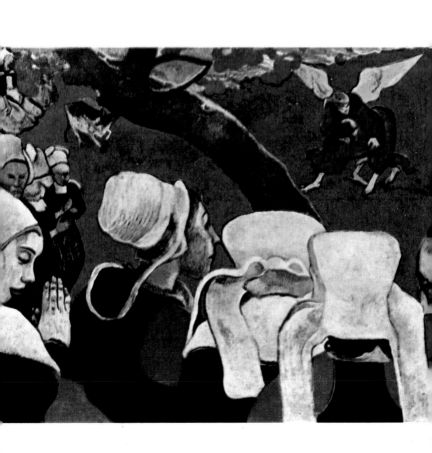

Gauguin 88

18

19

22 →

20

21

Aita tamari vahine Judith te parari

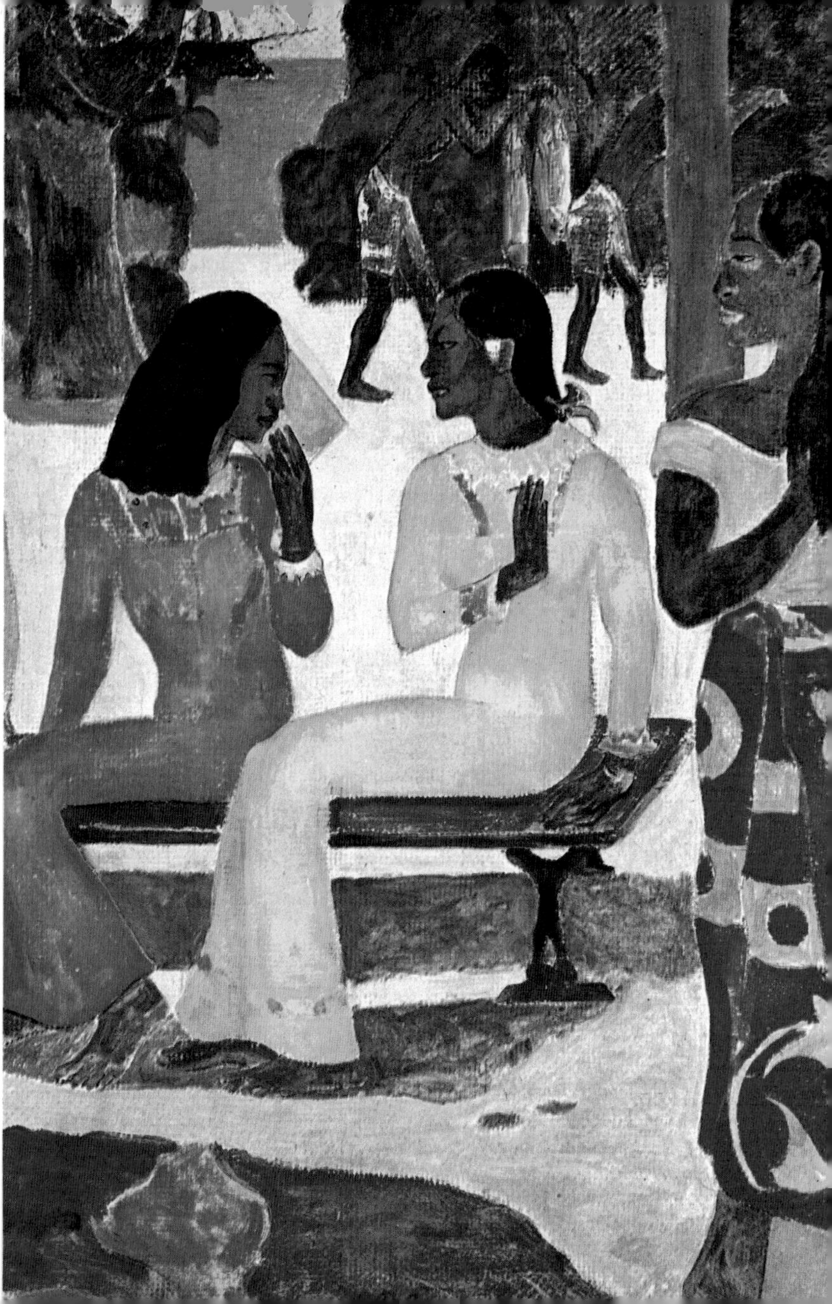

47

48

49

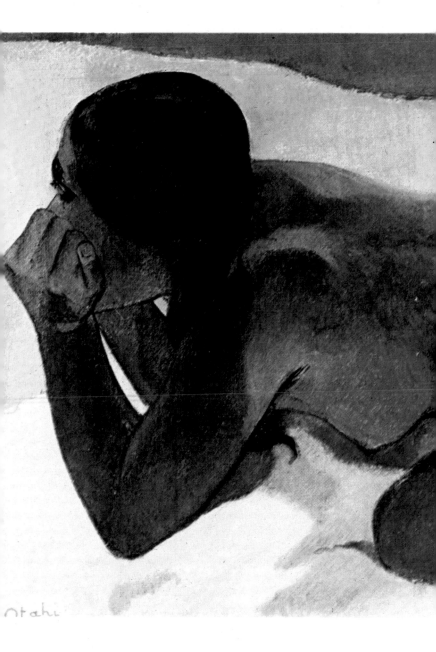

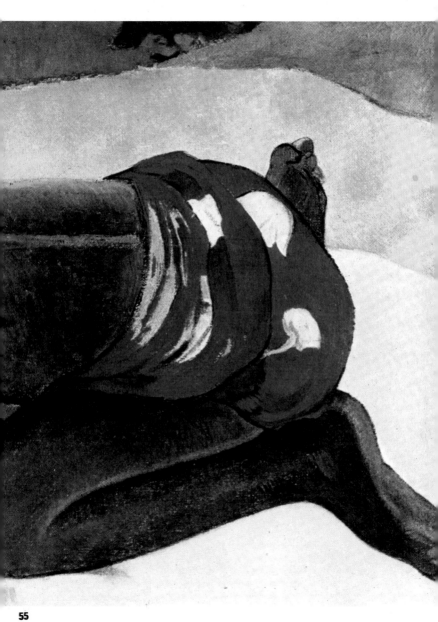

62 →

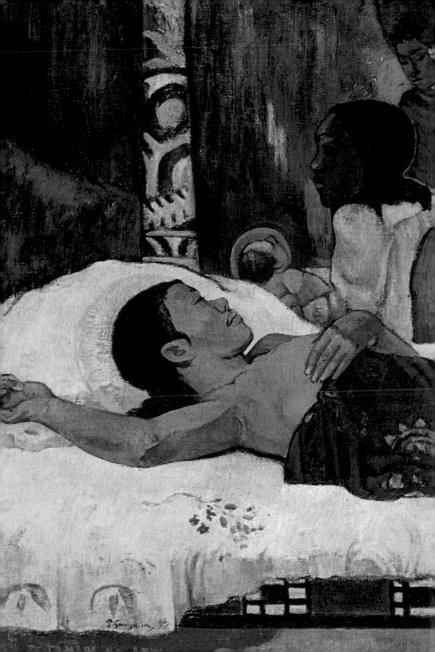

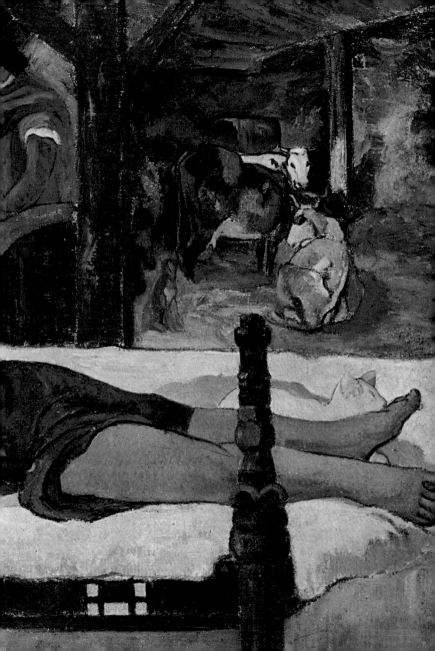

NAVE NAVE MAHANA

VAÏRUMATI
92

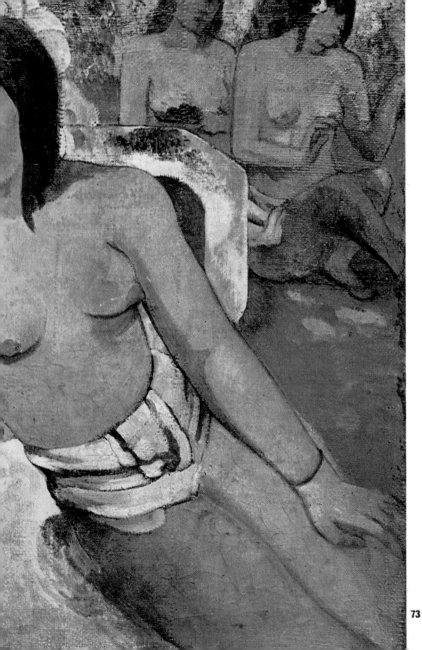

73

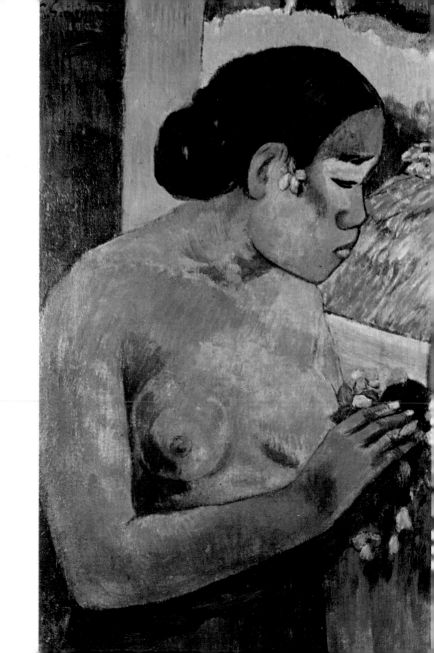

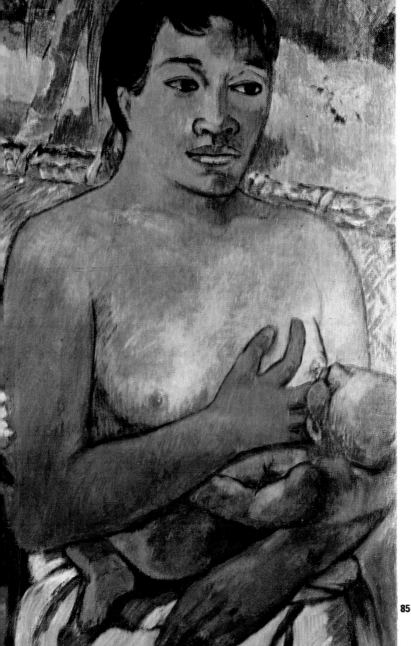